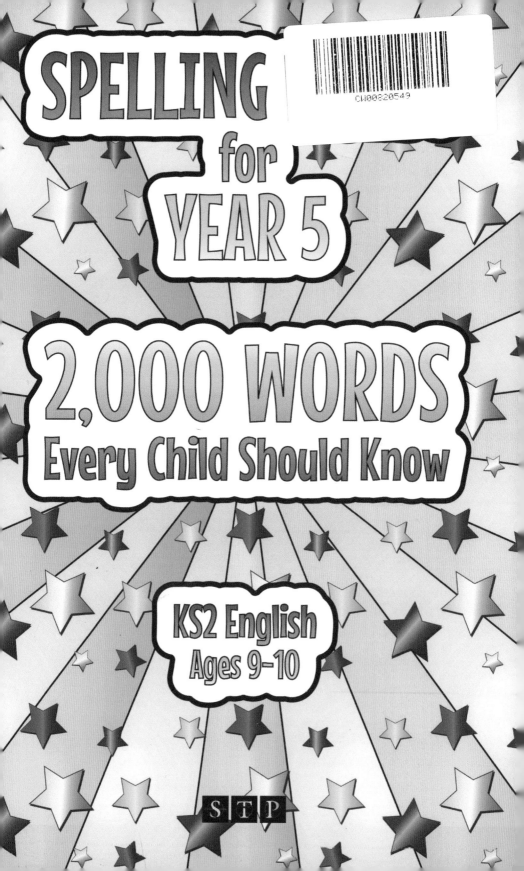

SPELLING for YEAR 5

2,000 WORDS
Every Child Should Know

KS2 English
Ages 9-10

STP

ABOUT THIS BOOK

Using a **fresh approach** to spellings lists, this illustrated collection of Spelling Words is designed **to make spelling fun** for your child whilst ensuring they master essential spelling rules covered by the end of Year 5.

Containing **2,000** carefully selected **level-appropriate** words, this book is made up of **70** Themed Spellings Lists that

- Have **brightly-coloured illustrated backgrounds** and **engaging titles**
- Cover **loads of topics** that **actually interest children** such as Creepy Crawlies, Fairy Tales, and Sports
- Relate to other **areas covered at school** like maths, Greek mythology, and astronomy
- Target **key words that children overuse** (e.g. 'said', 'bad', and 'nice')
- Quietly introduce **specific areas of spelling** that children need to know (e.g. using prefixes and suffixes, doubling consonants, and including silent letters)
- Are made up of **25 to 30 words each**

HOW TO USE IT

All the **lists are self-contained**, so you can work through them **in order**, or, you can dip in to use them for **focused practice**. And, as these lists are themed, they are **also a useful resource** for a range of **writing projects and exercises**.

For your convenience, an **Index** to the **spelling rules, patterns, and themed areas** dealt with by each of the lists is included at the **back of the book** on page 40.

Published by STP Books
An imprint of Swot Tots Publishing Ltd
Kemp House
152-160 City Road
London EC1V 2NX

www.swottotspublishing.com

Text, design, illustrations and layout © Swot Tots Publishing Ltd
First published 2020

Swot Tots Publishing Ltd have asserted their moral right under the Copyright, Designs and Patents Act, 1988, to be identified as the author of this work.

Typeset, cover design, and inside concept design by Swot Tots Publishing Ltd.

British Library Cataloguing-in-Publication Data. A catalogue record for this book is available from the British Library.

ISBN 978-1-912956-18-0

CONTENTS

CONTENTS Cont.

DIS- THE DISOBEDIENT

disable	discolour	disinfect
disadvantage	discomfort	dismissal
disagree	disconnect	disobey
disallow	discontinued	disorderly
disappear	discount	disoriented
disappoint	discourage	disown
disapprove	discourteous	disregard
disarm	disembarked	disrespectful
disassemble	disenchanted	disruption
disbelief	dishonour	dissatisfied

That Doesn't Look Right

accident	developing	opportunity
attached	dictionary	probably
awkward	explanation	recognise
bruised	favourite	recommend
category	forty	signature
cemetery	harassed	sincere
committee	identity	tomorrow
criticises	necessary	twelfth
definite	occasion	variety
determined	occupied	Wednesday

Creepy Crawlies

alighting	drone	millipede
antennae	fluttering	mosquito
arthropod	flying	moth
beetle	gnat	pollination
bluebottle	hatching	pupa
butterfly	infesting	spider
buzzing	insect	spinning
caterpillar	insecticide	stinging
centipede	larva	swarming
crawling	maggot	winged

Birds Of A Feather

albatross	cygnet	ibis
avian	flamingo	migration
beak	fledgling	nestling
caged	flightless	ostrich
camouflage	fowl	peck
caw	gosling	penguin
cheep	hatch	pheasant
chirp	hiss	plumage
claws	hoot	poultry
cluck	hummingbird	wading

It's All Greek To Me

anecdote	dynasty	prophet
anonymous	economy	prototype
arachnid	epic	synopsis
barometer	epidemic	theatre
chronic	kaleidoscope	tragedy
comedy	metropolis	
cosmopolitan	Neolithic	
cyclone	pandemic	
democracy	periscope	
dynamite	philosophy	

Oh? Ow? Or? Ooh?

although	enough	sourdough
borough	forethought	thorough
bough	fought	thoroughfare
bought	furlough	though
breakthrough	hiccough	thought
brought	nought	through
cough	ought	throughout
dough	plough	tough
doughnut	rough	trough
drought	sought	wrought

Good Heavens!

asteroid	cosmos	planet
astronaut	density	solar
astronomer	eclipse	solstice
astronomy	flare	supernova
black hole	galactic	universe
celestial	galaxy	
cluster	gravity	
comet	lunar	
constellation	meteor	
cosmic	orbit	

Silent, But Deadly

archaeologist	fascinated	receipt
biscuits	gnashed	rhymes
business	guarantees	rustling
campaigning	island	scent
catacombs	knapsack	solemnly
chemicals	lamb	succumbed
cologne	muscle	thistle
debt	nuisance	vehicles
disguise	pneumonia	wreck
doubts	queued	wrinkled

De- The Detached

deactivate
debrief
decamp
decelerate
decertify
declassify
decode
decompose
decrease *increase*
deface

defang
deflate
deforest
deform
defraud
defrost
defuse
degrease
dehumanize
dehydrate

demote
demystify
deport
depose
derail
deselect
detach
dethrone
devalue
devolve

Was That 'I' Before 'E'...

aliens
anxiety
barrier
believe
besieged
briefcase
brigadier
cashier
client
convenient

died
diesel
disobedient
fiend
fierce
friend
glacier
gondolier
grieved
hygiene

ingredient
lieutenant
niece
orient
pieces
pierce
quiet
relieved
shield
yield

...Or 'E' Before 'I'?

beige	freight	reindeer
being	height	reins
counterfeit	heinous	seized
decaffeinated	heist	sleigh
eiderdown	leisure	sovereign
eighteenth	neigh	theirs
either	neighbourhood	unveiling
feisty	poltergeist	vein
foreign	protein	weight
forfeit	reign	well-received

All In A Day's Work

accountant	illustrator	psychiatrist
architect	journalist	secretary
barrister	lawyer	software developer
beautician	lecturer	solicitor
chef	librarian	waiter
curator	make-up artist	
electrician	mechanic	
engineer	pharmacist	
gardener	photographer	
graphic designer	plumber	

Slam Dunk!

amateur	event	rivalry
arena	exhibition match	season
athlete	fitness	spectator
captain	foul	sport
championship	league	stadium
coach	match	success
competition	participate	title
competitor	pitch	tournament
court	professional	trainer
defeat	referee	umpire

They Yelled

Hi

barked	howled	shrilled
bellowed	jeered	squawked
booed	projected	thundered
called	raged	whooped
cheered	ranted	yelled
clamoured	roared	
cried	screamed	
hailed	screeched	
heckled	shouted	
hollered	shrieked	

We Said

added	expressed	reported
advised	informed	said
affirmed	insisted	spoke
agreed	maintained	stated
announced	mentioned	suggested
claimed	narrated	
commented	noted	
declared	observed	
described	related	
explained	remarked	

Too Cool For School

assistant	learning	subjects
curriculum	lenient	syllabus
department	obedient	teacher
detention	primary	timetable
discipline	reception	understand
education	regulations	
examination	satchel	
head teacher	secondary	
instruction	stationery	
knowledge	strict	

Do The Maths

addition	decimal	prime
area	diagonal	protractor
arithmetic	diameter	radius
brackets	division	ratio
calculation	factors	reflection
calculator	geometry	rotation
centimetre	horizontal	sequence
circumference	minus	subtraction
clockwise	multiplication	surface
compass	numeral	vertical

All Roads Lead To Rome

abdomen	extreme	journal
accuse	famine	laboratory
celebrity	ferocious	medieval
certificate	festival	pilgrim
condense	fortunate	secure
confide	funeral	
digit	gladiator	
domestic	gracious	
equator	hibernate	
external	image	

And Then...And Then...

another	furthermore	therefore
besides	generally	third
consequently	however	unlike
despite	in addition	while
even if	lastly	yet
even though	nevertheless	
fifth	next	
finally	second	
first	similarly	
fourth	subsequently	

Happy Endings I

accurate	hesitate	motivate
dedicate	imitate	narrate
donate	indicate	operate
elevate	inflate	populate
elongate	initiate	renovate
emigrate	isolate	rotate
equate	liberate	salivate
estimate	locate	separate
evacuate	migrate	vacate
fixate	moderate	validate

Back To Square One

acute	heptagon	quadrilateral
circular	hexagon	rectangle
concave	isosceles	rhombus
conical	obtuse	right-angled
convex	octagon	scalene
crescent	parallelogram	sphere
cuboid	pentagon	square
cylindrical	polygon	symmetrical
ellipse	prism	trapezium
equilateral	pyramid	triangle

Bookworms' Corner

autobiography	genre	novel
best seller	gripping	novella
best-selling	hardback	paperback
biography	lengthy	secondary character
boring	literature	story
catalogue	main character	suspense
classic	memoir	thrilling
description	mystery	tome
dialogue	narrative	villain
fiction	non-fiction	volume

It's All Good

acceptable	favourable	satisfying
admirable	fine	sound
advantageous	fitting	suitable
agreeable	helpful	super
competent	honourable	superb
enjoyable	marvellous	superior
excellent	pleasing	terrific
exceptional	positive	useful
exemplary	principled	wonderful
fantastic	satisfactory	worthy

Bad To The Bone

appalling	dreadful	poor
contaminated	faulty	rancid
corrupt	harmful	rotten
criminal	hurtful	shameful
damaging	inadequate	sinful
decayed	inferior	spoilt
defective	mediocre	unpleasant
destructive	mouldy	vile
disgraceful	nasty	weak
dishonest	offensive	wicked

DO Be...

adventurous	energetic	loyal
ambitious	enthusiastic	mature
amusing	fun-loving	polite
calm	hard-working	reliable
confident	honest	responsible
co-operative	humorous	sensible
courageous	imaginative	sociable
creative	independent	supportive
daring	intelligent	tolerant
decisive	inventive	witty

DON'T Be...

boastful	disorganised	lazy
bullying	fussy	nosy
conceited	gossipy	proud
controlling	greedy	reckless
cowardly	haughty	selfish
demanding	hypocritical	spoiled
dependent	immoral	stingy
devious	intolerant	uncooperative
disagreeable	irresponsible	undiplomatic
disloyal	jealous	ungrateful

Oh La La!

baguette
bonbon
chandelier
chariot
croissant
décor
domain
dossier
embassy
encourage

fiancé
fiancée
frontier
griddle
grill
gutter
journey
judgement
mayonnaise
meringue

parachute
portrait
queue
spinach
vinegar

A Diamond In The Rough

adornment
amethyst
aquamarine
crystal
dazzle
diamond
emerald
gems
jewellery
lapis lazuli

lustre
moonstone
opal
pearl
precious
quartz
ruby
sapphire
shine
solitaire

sparkle
topaz
translucent
turquoise
zircon

Double Trouble

acquitted	formatted	quitting
babysitter	hopping	referral
begging	inferred	shipping
beginning	knitting	strummed
bragging	nagging	transmitted
conferred	occurring	
deferral	outwitted	
emitting	planning	
equipped	preferred	
forgetting	propping	

Tech-Savvy

access	hardware	security
artificial intelligence	identity theft	signal
Bluetooth	innovation	social media
broadband	integrate	software
browser	internet	technology
computer	network	upload
digital	password	virtual reality
download	pixel	virus
glitch	processor	website
graphics	profile	wireless

No Place Like Home I

apartment	hermitage	rectory
barracks	maisonette	semi-detached
bungalow	manor	tenement
cabin	manse	town house
chalet	mansion	villa
château	monastery	
convent	nunnery	
cottage	orphanage	
flat	palace	
grange	ranch	

Circles Of Friends

assembly	crew	squad
audience	crowd	staff
bench	gang	throng
board	gathering	tribe
choir	horde	troupe
circle	household	
clan	majority	
community	minority	
congregation	population	
coven	rabble	

As Happy As A Lark

bouncy	glad	pleased
bubbly	gleeful	radiant
carefree	gratified	rapturous
cheerful	jolly	satisfied
content	jovial	smiling
contented	joyful	sunny
delighted	joyous	unconcerned
ecstatic	light-hearted	untroubled
elated	merry	unworried
euphoric	overjoyed	upbeat

COLOUR CODING

baby-blue	lime-green	sea-green
bottle green	milk-white	shocking pink
Day-Glo	navy blue	sky-blue
eggshell	nut-brown	snow-white
electric blue	off-white	straw-coloured
flesh-coloured	pea green	
ice blue	peacock blue	
iron-grey	pitch-black	
jet-black	rose-coloured	
lily-white	royal blue	

Mis- The Mistaken

misaddress
misalign
misapplied
misbehave
miscalculate
miscount
misdial
misdirection
misfit
misgovern

misguide
mishandle
misheard
misjudged
mislabel
mislaid
mislead
mismatch
misplaced
misprint

mispronounce
misremember
misreport
misshaped
misspeak
misspelled
misspelt
mistranslate
mistreatment
mistrustful

Putting Down Roots I

antibiotic
antibodies
anticlimax
anticlockwise
antifreeze
antihero
anti-hero
anti-inflammatory
antiseptic
antisocial

antitheft
anti-theft
antivirus
biannual
biceps
bicultural
bicycles
bilingual
bimonthly
binoculars

bisect
telecom
telegram
telegraph
telephone
teleport
telescope
telescopic
televise
television

MICE, NOT MOUSES

appendix	goose	series (s)
appendices	geese	series (p)
cactus	louse	sheep (s)
cacti	lice	sheep (p)
child	mice	this
children	mouse	these
deer (s)	ox	tooth
deer (p)	oxen	teeth
foot	person	woman
feet	people	women

YUMMY!

baklava	guacamole	pizza
biryani	kofta	pommes frites
borscht	lasagna	pretzel
canapé	milkshake	quesadilla
chocolate chip cookie	miso soup	quiche
chutney	moussaka	soufflé
crème caramel	naan	spaghetti
fajita	nachos	spring rolls
falafel	pad Thai	tofu
fondue	pavlova	tortilla

All Year Round

arctic	growth	sleet
autumn	harvest	spring
autumnal	heatwave	stubble
blizzard	icicle	summer
blooming	leafless	summery
blossom	mowing	temperature
buds	polar	wilt
falling	reaping	winter
flourishing	seasonal	wintery
fragrant	shoots	withering

Tick, Tock, Tick, Tock...

ancient	fortnight	monthly
anniversary	generation	prehistoric
annual	hours	promptly
centenary	jubilee	punctual
centennial	millennial	regularly
century	millennium	seconds
chronological	minutes	stopwatch
daily	modern	weekend
decade	moment	weekly
era	momentarily	yearly

No Place Like Home II

aquarium	hive	sett
barn	hole	shed
burrow	hutch	stable
cave	kennel	sty
coop	lair	web
den	lodge	
drey	nest	
earth	pasture	
eyrie	pen	
hill	pond	

Packs Of Wolves

army	herd	school
band	litter	shoal
barrel	menagerie	swarm
brood	mob	team
colony	murder	troop
covey	pack	
drove	parliament	
family	plague	
flock	pod	
gaggle	pride	

Run Of The Mill

accepted	general	stock
accustomed	habitual	traditional
average	humdrum	typical
characteristic	normal	unexceptional
common	ordinary	unremarkable
customary	predictable	
established	recognized	
everyday	regular	
expected	routine	
familiar	standard	

Out Of The Ordinary

abnormal	scarce	unique
bizarre	singular	unorthodox
curious	special	unprecedented
different	strange	unusual
distinctive	striking	weird
eccentric	surprising	
extraordinary	uncommon	
infrequent	unconventional	
peculiar	unexpected	
remarkable	unfamiliar	

ONCE UPON A TIME...

cobbler	gremlin	pirate
dragon	hobbit	pixie
dwarf	knight	puppet
elf	leprechaun	sprite
fairy	mayor	squire
fairy godmother	mermaid	stepmother
genie	minstrel	stepsister
giant	monster	townsfolk
gnome	ogre	troll
goblin	peasant	woodsman

...In A Land Far, Far Away

battled	enchanted	remote
captive	eternal	rescue
cast	evil	rightful
castle	fearsome	slumber
curse	hateful	succession
damsel	humble	tower
distress	imprisoned	transform
drawbridge	mischievous	trapped
dungeon	moral	treasure
enchained	naughty	trickery

Over- The Overlooked

overbearing	overfeed	overrun
overbook	overflowing	oversee
overbuy	overheat	overshadow
overcast	overindulgence	oversleep
overcome	overlap	overspend
overcook	overlook	overthrow
overdo	overlord	overtime
overdrive	overnight	overturn
overdue	overpay	overuse
overexcite	overprice	overweight

Water, Water Everywhere...

ashore	freshwater	saltwater
bobbing	gulf	seabed
buoy	harbour	sinking
coastal	lapping	source
current	marine	swelling
delta	maritime	tidal
downstream	nautical	trawler
erosion	navigate	upstream
fishermen	overboard	waves
flood	plunging	whaling

...AND NOT A DROP TO DRINK

arid	inhospitable	shimmering
barren	mirage	solitary
Bedouin	nomads	sparse
boundless	oasis	stony
camel	palm tree	stretching
dehydrated	parched	sun-baked
desert	rugged	thirst
dromedary	Sahara	uninhabited
dune	sandstorm	wasteland
horizon	scorched	wilderness

Happy Endings II

advertise	idealise	socialise
baptise	idolise	specialise
capitalise	itemise	standardise
colonise	magnetise	stylise
criticise	modernise	summarise
demonise	optimise	terrorise
dramatise	oxidise	utilise
familiarise	personalise	vaporise
finalise	publicise	visualise
hospitalise	sanitise	vocalise

Not Just A Pretty Face

bearded	frown	round
brow	glowing	ruddy
cheekbones	grimace	sallow
complexion	grin	scowl
craggy	handsome	smile
dimples	healthy	smirk
expression	heart-shaped	suntanned
features	lined	unshaven
forehead	oval	visage
freckles	pale	wince

I HEARD THAT!

audible	crash	rattle
aural	creak	ring
bang	deafening	shatter
blast	drip	slam
boom	echo	swish
chime	gurgle	thunderous
clatter	muffled	tinkle
clink	noise	whir
clunk	piercing	whoosh
crackle	racket	zoom

What Can You See?

afar	flicker	peer
behold	gleaming	plainly
blurry	glimmer	shade
candlelight	glimpsed	shadowy
darkness	gloom	shining
dimly	haze	sight
distance	mist	silhouette
distinctly	moonlight	spotted
dusky	murky	spy
faded	peep	sunlight

This Feels...

bumpy	glassy	sharp
burning	greasy	smooth
chafe	icy	sore
coarse	inflexible	stroke
damp	jagged	tactile
delicately	lightly	tenderly
dry	lukewarm	tickled
fingertip	moist	uneven
furry	oily	velvety
gently	rubbed	warmth

These Taste...

appetite	famished	peckish
beverage	flavour	ravenous
bitter	garnish	relish
catering	gorge	seasoned
chewed	gulped	sensation
crispy	indulgence	sipping
cuisine	inedible	sour
delicacy	nutrition	sugary
dietary	organic	undercooked
edible	palate	zest

What's That Smell?

aroma	hint	puff
bouquet	incense	pungent
breathe	inhale	reek
breeze	musk	sneeze
detect	musty	sniff
drift	odd	stench
faint	odour	stink
float	overpowering	trace
floral	overwhelming	waft
fragrance	perfume	whiff

Re- The Repetitive

reacquaint
react
reallocated
reapplied
reassurance
reboot
rebuilt
reclaim
reconnect
reconsider

recur
recurring
redecorate
redeliver
redesigned
redirect
redouble
re-editing
re-elected
re-employ

re-enter
re-evaluation
re-examining
refill
reformed
replant
replay
reselect
retake
review

IT'S A BIG DEAL!

central
chief
critical
crucial
distinguished
eminent
essential
esteemed
grave
key

landmark
main
major
momentous
monumental
notable
noted
noteworthy
outstanding
paramount

principal
priority
relevant
serious
significant
urgent
valuable
valued
vital
weighty

Neither Here Nor There

immaterial	marginal	smaller
incidental	meagre	subordinate
inconsequential	minor	subsidiary
inconsiderable	negligible	trifling
insignificant	non-essential	trivial
insubstantial	optional	unclassified
irrelevant	petty	unimportant
junior	second-class	unknown
lesser	slight	unnecessary
light	small	worthless

Happy Endings III

amplify	glorify	petrify
beautify	gratify	purify
clarify	horrify	qualify
classify	identify	rectify
dignify	intensify	simplify
disqualify	justify	specify
diversify	magnify	terrify
electrify	modify	testify
exemplify	notify	unify
falsify	pacify	verify

Him & Her

abbot	emperor	master
abbess	empress	mistress
bridegroom	heir	prince
bride	heiress	princess
earl	hero	shepherd
countess	heroine	shepherdess
sire	lord	steward
dam	lady	stewardess
duke	manservant	sultan
duchess	maidservant	sultana

All Fired Up!

agog	fanatical	sparkling
animated	fiery	stirred
ardent	impassioned	thrilled
avid	impatient	vigorous
buoyant	intense	wholehearted
committed	intent	
eager	interested	
earnest	keen	
exhilarated	passionate	
expectant	ready	

Be Nice!

affectionate

amiable

big-hearted

caring

charitable

compassionate

considerate

courteous

friendly

generous

genial

gentle

good-hearted

good-natured

hospitable

humane

kindly

loving

merciful

mild

neighbourly

obliging

patient

selfless

sympathetic

tactful

thoughtful

understanding

unselfish

warm

ZEUS & CO.

ambrosia

Argonaut

centaur

chimera

cyclops

demi-god

Elysian Fields

fate

gorgon

Hades

harpy

hydra

immortal

minotaur

mortal

Mount Olympus

muse

nectar

nymph

Olympian

oracle

pantheon

prophecy

prophetic

revenge

satyr

siren

soothsayer

Trojan Horse

underworld

Lost In The Mists Of Time

account	fable	profane
afterlife	folklore	runes
allegory	history	sacred
ancestors	holy	saga
antiquity	interpretation	scrolls
civilization	legend	supernatural
culture	monuments	tablets
deity	myth	tale
divinity	origins	temples
explanations	pagan	traditions

A Mean Streak

brutal	inhumane	snide
callous	insensitive	spiteful
cold-hearted	malevolent	thoughtless
cruel	malicious	uncaring
cutting	mean	unfeeling
hard-hearted	merciless	unfriendly
harsh	painful	unkind
heartless	pitiless	unsympathetic
inconsiderate	remorseless	vicious
inhuman	ruthless	vindictive

Putting Down Roots II

subcontinent	subtext	superhero
subeditor	subtitle	superhuman
subhuman	subtotal	superman
sublet	subtract	supermarket
submarine	suburb	superrich
submenu	suburban	supersede
submerge	subvert	supersize
subplot	subway	superstar
subset	superbug	superstore
subside	superglue	supervise

Scared To Death

afraid	intimidated	skittish
alarmed	jittery	spooked
anxious	jumpy	startled
apprehensive	nervous	tense
dismayed	panicked	terrified
disturbed	panic-stricken	uneasy
fearful	petrified	unnerved
frightened	quivery	unsettled
hesitant	scared	uptight
horrified	shaky	worried

DOWN IN THE DUMPS

anguished	distressed	melancholic
cheerless	down	miserable
crestfallen	downcast	mournful
crushed	forlorn	sorrowful
dejected	gloomy	tearful
demoralized	glum	unhappy
depressed	grieving	upset
despairing	heartbroken	woebegone
dismal	hopeless	woeful
dispirited	joyless	wretched

SEEING RED

aggravated	fuming	mad
aggrieved	furious	outraged
annoyed	grouchy	peeved
bad-tempered	grumpy	provoked
cross	ill-tempered	raging
crotchety	incensed	seething
disgruntled	indignant	sullen
displeased	infuriated	surly
enraged	irritable	vexed
exasperated	irritated	wrathful

INDEX

In the following entries, the letter 'A' refers to the upper list on the page, while 'B' refers to the lower one.

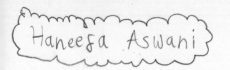
Haneefa Aswani

Printed in Great Britain
by Amazon